WAR & PEACE

OR *The Cat Should Sleep Where She Wants*

WAR & PEACE

OR *The Cat Should Sleep Where She Wants*

BARBARA COLES

LIP PUBS TRADE PAPERBACKS
CROCKETT, CALIFORNIA

To my mother, Dorothy Coles: the cat lady I aspire to, gracious, generous, tolerant. So many cats can't be wrong.

ANY ERRORS OF HEBREW
OR LATIN TRANSLATION
ARE SQUISHY'S.
I DO NOT TRANSLATE;
I TRANSCEND.

—*The Cat*

HOW BEAUTIFUL TO DO
NOTHING, AND THEN REST
AFTERWARD.

—*Spanish Proverb*

WAR & PEACE

OR *The Cat Should Sleep Where She Wants*

Dizzy

I helped Squishy take a nap after lunch today. She even thanked me for keeping her lap warm, although I was happy to do it.

She woke up this morning with something she calls dizziness. When she has dizziness, she touches the walls, walks with dignity, like a cat, and moans now and again. She will do a little dance, an unsteady cross step, until she touches a wall and the dance stops.

Squishy says her ears cause her dizziness, not the colored water that smells like fiery tongs to the eyes. I don't see how that can be, when her ears are well protected by her silky fur, but she's generally truthful, so I'll take her word for it.

But let me introduce myself. Besides being queen of the universe, I am called the cream-colored cat, Kitty, Ouch, Stop That! and Fluffy, Destroyer of Nations. Having so many names is a sign of my overarching importance to my minions. (I love that word, minions. Roll it around on your tongue: shout it out—MINIONS—whisper it—minions—always the perfect combination of sound and meaning.) I am beautiful in the extreme, with long cream-colored fur and crystal blue eyes. The fluffiness of my tail—well, it is unequaled.

Especially by the brick-like tabby person who lives outside the back door. She is also called kitty, but it is "kitty," not Kitty, like me. She may have a curl at the end of her spiky little tail that Squishy finds "cute," but let me ask you—who is on the porch, and who is helping dizzy minions take naps?

Enough about me—for now.

Squishy did only three important things today besides our nap. She disappeared with Popcorn, the boy minion of the family, as she does most mornings, and returned without him so we could have the house all to ourselves. Then, she put foods all together in a big black pot to cook all day, including some spectacular-smelling beefy bits. She tossed in some potatoes, carrots, and onions as well. I have no objection to these things, but why bother when you have beefy bits?

The last thing she did was to build a fire. Rumble usually does this, but in a pinch, Squishy can do it. Sometimes she hisses and yowls when the fire fights back, but today she purred at its leaping and smiling, before she sat down with a thump.

When she closed her eyes in the chair by the fire, I was ready to help. She didn't move for two hours. Lovely. She didn't really need to thank me, but Squishy can be very thoughtful that way, dizzy or not.

Glove

I have a new hobby this week, vital for the safety of my minions. It is similar to my old hobbies of chasing rubber bands and the plastic tops of milk cartons, and batting the broccoli spears Popcorn sometimes drops accidentally on purpose. But if I grab this new thing, it might grab back. This hobby is dangerous. Let me explain.

Squishy is furless, although I don't hold it against her. On the other hand, Rumble, the minion who builds fires, has a pelt any cat would be proud of, that is, if the cat didn't possess the perfection of a dream of a cloud of a coat like I have.

It's not an easy task to live up to fur like mine. I've been known to stop whatever I'm doing, even gazing at birds, to see to the condition of my coat. A few licks won't do it either—with its density and fluffiness, my coat needs the single-minded concentration of the lioness hunting the gazelle. My tongue is the tongue of a fur master, well-trained, skilled, and rougher than any other tongue in the house. Or outside of it: I would sneer at the tongue of the outdoor tabby person, with her short little stripy coat, but it would be beneath me. Squishy says...

Wait. Where was I?

Yes, Squishy is furless, so her parts get cold. She and the other minions put on clothes to keep them warm, even in the house. Sometimes they need many layers, and this leads me to my new hobby. Squishy has hand-shaped clothes; when her hands are not in them, they are clothes of absolute evil.

Usually, Squishy confines them to a drawer in the mudroom, caged and chained, I think. But lately, she's become complacent, tossing them in the direction of her purse, where they are free to roam. With those prehensile digits, black as an outdoor cat's soul, the damage they could do...well, if I could shudder to think of the consequences, I would.

Squishy, Rumble and Popcorn seem unaware of the impending disaster of the spider garb. Squishy even (and I blush for her) left two pairs free the other day. Four of these devil clothes out at once! I don't shudder, but I can shake my head at this negligence, so...I shake my head. But I don't shirk, so I got busy.

First, I assessed the danger; they looked inert, but I wasn't fooled. I leaped, hooking one with my claws and flinging it in the air. The other dropped from the purse to the floor and lay there, preparing the counter-attack. I split their forces by running down the hallway with the first one in my mouth. As it struggled, I maintained my grip on one writhing finger.

Outside the boy's room, it twisted free and jumped for my head, its leathery black hide like the maw of the cat carrier of doom. I couldn't let it get to Popcorn (who entertains me by swinging his arms around and making pew-pew noises, and sometimes feeds me) so I pounced. I crushed it and smacked it and wrung it and clawed it. Finally, just as I was getting bored, it died.

I took it, no longer struggling, under the kitchen table. Squishy saw me resting with one finger-tip in my mouth. She said, "My glove!" and began to laugh. I had saved her from danger. She could carry on with her oblivious, carefree life.

The other day, I took on the other black enemy and a multicolored fuzzy one. I do my duty, protecting those unable to protect themselves.

Now I have a name for evil, and that name is glove.

Mat

Just when I think my minions understand that they shouldn't change anything in my house, they add a new level of tension to my already fraught existence.

A few weeks ago, I heard Rumble talking about "new door mats." Squishy was passionate in her agreement, so I thought they were talking about me, and how perhaps they should stop at the door mat and bow three times before entering my presence.

Or maybe they were talking about flattening that tabby interloper into something I could sleep on. I waited to see if a small tiger-striped rug would appear for my pleasure. Nothing happened, but Squishy can be lackadaisical about her work, and Rumble is away from home a lot. I began to forget about it.

But, oh, when I tried to step out the side door yesterday! Staring at me was a crescent-shaped danger in the form of a new, pebbly door mat. I reeled—shock, dismay, anger!

At the front door, another new mat! At the porch door, another! What a time for Squishy to be industrious, instead of forgetting about the cockamamie ideas she and Rumble have, like she usually does.

The porch mat even had the nerve to say "Wipe Your Paws." As if I would fall into the trap of setting a paw on a door mat.

I've always made it my practice to avoid door mats, those yawning caverns of danger. You can get in a door without stepping on them if you plan your strategy well and stiffen your tail with courage. Or catch them when they're sleeping, which they do on warm afternoons.

If you leap as high as you can over one corner, you won't be sucked into the door mat vortex of destruction. You have to time it right, though. The best time is when a minion has been holding the door open for you for three to four minutes. Human complaints lull door mats into insensibility.

Sometimes my minions, looking out for my safety, shut the door before I jump, and we try again later. When will it end? Today, door mats, tomorrow, what? The tabby gets to come inside? I've been too benevolent with my minions, too, too kind.

Counter

Back in the mists of a dim past, Squishy tried to discipline me. I would jump on the inviting expanse of the kitchen table, and she would try to shoo me off. I would leap onto the raised wooden counter that hid the dirty dishes from the family room, and she would clap her hands at me.

It worked a few times. But my shock wore off, and Squishy wore down. She gave it up, and I gained both the advantage and a vantage point for all sorts of interesting doings.

Rumble has a quirkiness that can sometimes be alarming and sometimes endearing, but always fascinating. He truly believes, as Squishy once believed about me, that Squishy can be disciplined.

Each evening, Rumble assembles his food for the next day. One joy of the wooden counter is that I can give him my benevolent surveillance, looking at him eye to eye.

"The cat is on the counter," he says. He drops this pronouncement like a catnip mouse in front of a feline, expecting Squishy to grab it and run. She, on the other hand, has learned much from me about toying with prey.

"Mmmm?" she lobs back, not looking up from her crossword puzzle.

He tries a more direct approach. "The cat shouldn't be on the counter."

Not looking up, still penciling more squares, she says, "No, she really shouldn't."

"She should get down."

"Push her off."

"I'd have to touch her."

"You could wash your hands."

Squishy never deviates from her distant sang-froid. Sometimes she makes me want to weep with pride.

A last, desperate volley comes from Rumble: "Can you do something about the cat?"

Deigning to glance up this time, Squishy returns fire. "She'll just jump up again."

Rumble gives up. He stares at me, and I get ready to jump if it becomes necessary. But years of training pay off, even with the most rock-headed of minions.

As he measures out his raisin and chocolate chip snack, he asks me, "Am I doing it right?"

A big question, a cosmic question, really. Yes, he's doing it right: the cat is amused.

Morning

This morning, as I do every morning, I checked out the porch door for the terrible tabby. She was still there, showing her low class by ignoring the insulting "Wipe Your Paws" door mat. She even meowed through the glass, as if she has any right to make demands on Squishy like I do.

Since Rumble has objections to sleeping with me—Rumble has objections to many reasonable things, as far as I can tell, like me on the kitchen table, tufts of silky cream-colored hair on the bottom of his pants, my need to be let in and out each morning ten times or so—so most of the time, I sleep in the mud room on a Winnie the Pooh quilt that once belonged to my girl, Cuddle. I have food, water and a necessary box, so it's not so bad, but I run and hide at bedtime as a matter of principle. The cat should sleep where she wants. It cannot be stressed enough: the cat should sleep where she wants.

Anyway, I sleep in the mudroom.

In the morning, when I hear Squishy on the stairs, I jump down from the windowsill of the mudroom—kadunk—and I'm ready at the door to be let out. When she opens the door, I walk out, stretch, and bless her with a morning meow as she runs her hand down my back. Most mornings, she tells me I'm sweet. Then I walk to the back door and check to see if a miracle has occurred. So far, in terms of miracles, I am an agnostic. The tabby remains.

I really don't know what possesses Squishy sometimes. For some reason, she thinks it's all right to open the porch door and let the tabby in. If I could find a way to stop that nonsense, I would, but so far nothing has worked. I used to bat at the furry trousers of that cat, but she either paid no attention or had the gall to turn around and bat back. Squishy would push me away with her foot and talk about my protective tendencies in the most insulting language, not only directing her comments to the stripey hillbilly, but doing it right in front of me.

After Squishy shows a sickening display of concern for the tabby pest's well-being, she feeds her first. I've come to believe it's because the best always takes the ultimate place, and the second-rate, the penultimate, in a sort of practice run, and not because the little lout will eat my food if given a chance, which is what Squishy says. Squishy is a simple soul and doesn't think these things through.

And this morning, as she has for a little while now, the tabby greeted me nose to nose, then insinuated herself under my chin to rub against me. I'm still startled when she does this, so startled I hardly have time to raise my paw to batting position before she's eeling her way somewhere else. It gives me such a strange feeling of doubt and discombobulation that I retreat to my food spot, sit down and wait with dignity, and let her abase herself with meows at Squishy's feet.

Life used to be so much simpler.

Cuddle

Today I wander the house, looking for my girl.

The rain is falling like sharp, slanted claws. Last night, a roar and banging above me made me look at the ceiling, and Squishy told Popcorn to come look. I jumped on the windowsill to look with them. Tiny white balls covered the ground, and the cold seeped past my coat. I almost felt sorry for the tabby pest outside, though it didn't stop me resenting it when Squishy set out a sleeping bag for her on her favorite chair and made coo-coo noises at her.

On days like this, I need all the comfort

my good life can offer. But in spite of Rumble stoking the fire to keep me warm and Squishy scratching my back as I complain about eating dry food and Popcorn fighting his screen wars safe at home, today I miss Cuddle.

Where has the sweetest of minions gone? I ask myself. What is she doing? Poor me, I think. Poor Cuddle, because she's without me. How can she be happy? I wander the house, hoping for Cuddle of a thousand pillows to come back to me, so I can tuck my head beneath her chin, curl up to nap, secure on her chest, and purr and purr and purr.

I know Cuddle is all right, because I hear Squishy on the phone, chirping or cooing with love. When she hums and pets with her voice, I know she's talking to Cuddle.

Sometimes, Squishy and I read in Cuddle's room, where all but one pillow are gone. The mountains and valleys of her life here are cleared away, and her room, where her comforting chaos reigned, idles from one week to the next.

I don't like it. I don't think it does Squishy much good, either.

Life wasn't perfect when Cuddle was here. Sometimes, she and Squishy hissed and scratched as if one were a fluffy goddess and the other a tabby upstart, but they didn't know who was what. Their yowling would send me scurrying under the coffee table in fear for my tail.

The worst was when Squishy's voice would go low and thunderous, and Cuddle would gather storms around her head that sent water down her face. The lightning would pound and pound, until, finally, all was said, and their ears were unstopped. The rain would gentle, their words would rise and fall. Squishy would hum her love again, and Cuddle would call her "Mommy."

Sometimes it took minutes, sometimes hours. Sometimes, weeks.

But I don't think that's why Cuddle left. For a long time, she has been as big as Squishy, a grown-up size. Like kittens need to leave their mothers to find their own minions, I think sometimes young minions have to leave home to find cats of their own. For Cuddle's sake, I hope it's not a tabby, but even I can't do anything about that.

I'm sad that Cuddle isn't mine anymore, after belonging to me for so many years, but I still have Squishy. Even Rumble and Popcorn can be a comfort to me in their own inadequate ways.

But today, while it rains, I want sweet Cuddle.

Backpack

Lolling on Popcorn's backpack, I am the queen of the world. No, I'm that already. Lolling on Popcorn's backpack, I am the queen of the universe. If cats had such a thing as a guilty pleasure, backpacks would be mine.

One day long ago, as I meditated and did deep breathing near Cuddle's backpack, I had an urge to drape myself over it. Then the necessity of rubbing it with my face struck me.

I wormed my head under the strap, bit the little plastic thingies, and butted my head and

nose on it. It had rough and rougher parts that felt sublime against my face. Each time Cuddle deserted me for the day, she slung this bag on her shoulder, and on it I smelled smells from an ocean of teenage minions: oily, herbal, flowery, over-heated, under-formed, anxious, giddy smells.

After ten minutes, I was full up with this heady mix, and I rested, laying my chin on the netted pencil holder, my paws embracing the fat bottom of the backpack.

When Rumble set his backpack on the floor one night, with its faint odor of chemicals and persnickety, fine-tuned machinery, shivers ran along my spine like mice on rafters, shivers and hair-on-end in the most delicious way possible. So again, I rubbed.

Popcorn, that good boy, now has two backpacks. One is like Cuddle's, with a youthful froth of odors. It is large, and I fight with it, pretending it is a big, scarred tom cat, who I bring to order with my feminine wiles and a good, swift whack in the chops. I especially enjoy chewing on the ends of the straps, which double as a big, scarred, tom cat's ears.

Popcorn's other backpack has only lived at our house for a few weeks. It leaves with Popcorn just once a week, for a game of what he calls "D and D." I've heard him say, "Dungeons and Dragons is the center of my life now!"

Squishy says, "I've got to take you to church more."

I say he needs to spend more time with me and get his priorities straight.

Inside this backpack are tiny figures that are almost human, but not quite. They all seem to have a large quantity of teeth and hair. If the backpack is open, I can fish them out and fight them, but it's more like fighting ugly mice than fighting tom cats. They skitter and snarl and, with their pugnacious personalities, make a nice change from rubber bands.

If Popcorn catches me at it, he grips his head and says "No, no, no!" He's concerned for my safety, I'm sure, and will do anything to protect me, even clap his hands and chase me under a chair. He says, "Those aren't mine!" as he does it. I don't know what that means, but it's a fun game.

The uncouth tabby ruffian has the unattractive habit of dribbling when she's scratched under the chin. I don't drool, but if ever I sank low enough, I know backpacks would be my drool of choice.

Desk

I'm helping Squishy write today. She has a tiny desk in a tiny nook, and I'm stretched out in front of her screen on a space the size of half a pillow. It's not comfortable, but it gives her something to aspire to, this vision of perfection before her, so I'll stay awhile. She likes it, I can tell, and I have nothing else to do anyway.

I don't know what the point of her writing is, especially when it seems to cause her such torment. While she sits at her desk, she mutters to herself. Strange things, alien to cat culture, like "Forge ahead! Produce! I am my own CEO!" Frequently, it's just "Damn it!"

I say give it up and sleep. Human nature, I've discovered, says otherwise.

They labor under the impression that what they do is Very Important. Yes, the cat must be fed, kept warm, and scratched behind the ears. A roof over the young minions' heads isn't a bad idea either, but beyond that, I just can't see the urgency. Especially this writing stuff.

Granted, it gives me an interest. I loll while Squishy's fingers clack over the keyboard. I watch her feet wiggle and twitch. I twine around her legs beneath the desk. It's easier than following her around the house, and much better than being left for the day—dare I say it—alone.

Sometimes, though, work at her desk makes her downright nasty. Those days, her fingers travel up into her hair. When I'm ready to leave the nook, I meow over and over and over, as is my right. Then she has been known to use the "S" word on me, which I know is a bad word, because she doesn't say it to Popcorn, Cuddle or Rumble.

"Shut up, cat!" she says. When the writing really drives her crazy, she might even use the other "S" word. "Shut up, you stupid cat!"

Then I am unrelenting in my demands, because someone needs to snap her out of this soul-consuming obsession. I should be her only obsession, and she knows it.

In the end, sighing and moaning, she gets up. I always win, though I know enough to avoid her feet on days like this.

I've moved to the bed now. Much more comfortable, and more helpful for making my little squeaky happy noises as I sleep. Squishy enjoyed having my silky guard hairs sweeping her fingers as she typed today, but I know my happy noises, as well as stretching in my sleep as my paws hug my nose, remind her every day that Very Important should always give way to Most Important.

Popcorn

One thing about Popcorn: you have to watch out for his feet.

Not only are they bigger than they used to be, but he seems not to know where they are. I think it's because his head is so far up in the clouds that his feet are just dimly theoretical to him. So if I want to go through a door, but Popcorn is coming through the same door, I retreat and say "No, after you. I insist." He tends not to hear me, which is why I don't make an issue of my right of "cat first." I value my ribs, and Popcorn would feel bad if he sent me aloft.

Popcorn spends much of his time fighting screen wars, which seem to provide him a rich and varied life. I always enjoy my minions who spend hours not moving much, so if Squishy's not at home, my favorite spot is reclining on the inch or two of seldom-disturbed papers next to the big computer, watching the expressions that fleet over Popcorn's face. With his legs folded up in the chair like a cricket's, he wiggles and yells. Although it's sometimes alarming, it couldn't be more entertaining.

He, like Squishy, writes things, but with greater determination and success and less tearing of hair. He reads them to Squishy and Rumble, and they laugh or shiver with dread, depending on the nature of his work for the day.

Popcorn is a good boy, even if his attitude to me, his lovely liege, is one of oblivious goodwill. He makes sure I am fed when Squishy can't. He yells at me now and then when I scratch the furniture, adding that certain something of danger and excitement I crave. On rare occasions, he pets me, one or two strokes, which is all the petting I really want anyway.

To reward him, I have walked onto his lap a time or two, even bypassing Squishy, to settle and purr. His reaction of stunned gratitude is all that I could wish for. He hardly breathes in order not to disturb me, and his hand on my back is always light and reverent.

But of all things, I appreciate Popcorn the most when he goes outside and paces beside our little road up the hill.

As he paces, he swings his arms as though cutting through swaths of enemies, leading me to believe that humans once had claws. He issues subdued battle cries so as not to alarm the cats, takes aim, and goes "pew, pew!" I don't know what this sound means, but the tabby pest and I agree in this one thing: no better way to spend a sunny afternoon exists than to curl up on our little lawn with paws tucked in, watching Popcorn swing his arms and go "pew, pew!" When we tire of watching, we hunt gophers and bugs, or each other, knowing Popcorn's antics will scare anything that might like to eat cats far, far away from us.

We may hunt and loll in safety, because Popcorn is near.

Other

I know Big Fluff says things about me. I don't blame her. She is a glowing cat who sleeps inside at night, and I am just a small tabby who has lived rough mostly.

I have outlived my mother and my sister, who lived rough all their lives, rougher than me because they did not know about persons who can be kind. I learned from my mother and sister that I must have holes and hideaways and be ever alert, because as we eat the small, so the large can eat us.

Person has been good to me. She speaks sweet to me and gives me soft, flavorful food morning and night. I trust her now so much that I will speak to her when I am very hungry to hurry her along. She says, "Yes, yes, I hear you." That is good, almost as good as food.

Now in the day, Person lets me inside to take naps. I choose mostly a bed under a table where there is not much coming and going, a little way up on a seat, a cave-like place and out of the way of Big Fluff. She is not nice to me sometimes and hits me until Person pushes her away and I can sleep in peace.

Big Fluff's hitting is just nonsense, so some days I walk right up to her and claim her with rubbing, especially when I am hungry. Oh, her surprise! Inside me, I find it funny that a little outdoor thing like me can make such a beauty pull her face back and turn her tail, out of my way.

And then, on the days I am so hungry, when I haven't been to the back door in a day or two, my patience for this swatting silliness is low. I ignore Big Fluff, pretending I can't see her anywhere around. She doesn't know what to think of that, I can tell you.

Other times, I let her bat my behind. She thinks she is queen then, and I am never hurt by it.

I think Big Fluff was an only kitten, because she doesn't know that when we are outside and I rush at her all puffed up, I am playing. She tries sometimes to play, rushing at me, but the rush is too fast and the look on her face so mean that I step back, not sure what she wants, until it is too late and she has lost the bravery to play with me. Someday, maybe we will understand each other.

I would like to stay inside at night, especially when the flat-faced tom comes around to eat from my bowl. He is loud, meowing at the door like he is king, but when Person comes to the door, he sneaks off like a mouse afraid to raise its head. I would laugh at him for it, except when he finds me and beats me up, it is not funny.

Person calls me many names, more and more as we know each other. Shiloh is the name some person gave me, and Person calls me that. It means "peace" and that is what I feel now when we are quiet together and she strokes me. She also calls me Shy-shy, in a high voice, which means I am about to get food. Sometimes, it is Curly, because of the curl at the end of my tail.

She calls me Pretty, too, even though I am just a tabby. I do have a white, white bib and white paws I keep bright with washing. My fur is short, but thick and soft with the good food I eat and the cold of winter.

Person is always gentle, even as she takes me from the seat I don't want to leave, all my claws gripping. She is good-good. She makes me think that someday, when I have learned what I need to learn, I will spend each night in safety.

Bella

Squishy has a new name for me. She thinks she's clever.

Thinking she's clever is Squishy's problem. The penchant, or need, for cleverness is what leads her to, yes, mock me sometimes. I know: if a person can mock me, then any of the higher virtues—truth, justice, the pursuit of lizards—are open to mockery.

Recently I have discovered that the little tabby goblin has a real name. I consider her name a mockery itself, because Shiloh is her name. This name, according to Squishy, means "peace."

Ha! Certainly not my peace. Just today the pest sashayed out of the living room, glanced at me and headed to her food plate for a snack. Even that phrase, "her food plate," implies she has weaseled her way into my territory. As she hunkered down to suck up the remains of her seafood paté, I eased my way close to her. I sat and wrapped my front paws in the cloak of my magnificent tail, adding to my air of otherworldly mystery and threat. Then I fixed her with a stink eye that should have chilled her bones.

I am the queen of such a stink eye, the diva, if you will, of menacing glances. Squishy, though lazy and emotionally fragile, is no coward—yet even Squishy recoils, shivering, when pinned in my burning glance.

But did the little idiot cat have the brains to know she should run howling from my presence? She did not. She turned her big, weird, amber eyes on me for a moment and went back to smacking away at her food. I found it hard to stomach her insensibility, so after staring one more icy moment for emphasis, I sashayed to my own food dish to drown the sorrows of this degenerate world. I lapped up a slug of water and worked out my tension with the crunch of Friskies Complete.

My original minion-given name was Sofia (given by those first unsatisfactory, pre-Squishy minions, who could not bear up under my perfection. I sent them packing.) Sofia is not a bad name, a name with an air of romance to it. I could be a Sofia, though never a Sophie. Sophie might suit the pest, indicating a gormless moron who spends her time with mice in barns or someone who might even sink so low as to play with dogs. Sofia reclines on red-tiled floors in the sun of a Spanish winter; Sophie is one who gets stuck by accident in the Spanish horses' oat bin.

Then I was Shelly, named by Cuddle. No.

Mostly, I am Kitty with a capital K. As I've said before though, I'm so important, I have many names: Miss Kitty, Missy, Kitty Blister (to show Cuddle and Popcorn's allegiance to me, as they are referred to as Sister Blister and Mister Blister), Mookie, the Queen, Fluff, Fluffy Destroyer of Nations, etc, etc. These names only hint at my great power. When Squishy is worked up by my terrible might, she calls upon my war names: You Devil, Damn Cat, Ouch, Let Go, Terrible Cat, Stop That.

Sometimes I'm called Idiot Cat and Stupid Cat when Squishy's having a nice change by doing actual work, and I supervise; mostly, however, these names come from Rumble, the blasphemer.

In any case, my new name, given me by Squishy in a moment of idiot humor, is Bella. According to her, Shiloh, meaning peace, deserves Bella, meaning war. I resent being tied to the tabby goof in any way, even by one twentieth of my given names, yet it is strangely appropriate. When I am spreading destruction by shredding the pink chair (yes, I'm sorry, they have a pink chair, upon the back of which I look stunning, by the way) or digging out strawberry hulls in the trash, Squishy invokes my war name at a high volume. The ensuing sense of power is exhilarating and I bolt up the stairs, claws tearing at the carpet with a ripping sound fearsome to the human ear. Squishy's favorite compliment to me at times like these is "Yikes!"

Squishy and I are having a quiet moment now, her tender strokes sending me to cat nirvana. She is chanting her love song to me, and I find it is also my war name: "Bel-la, Bel-la, Bel-la, lovely Bel-la."

As I give an idle yawn, as Squishy scratches behind my ears, her whispers tell me that Bella also means beautiful. Yes.

Squishy's so-called cleverness notwithstanding, I am, after all, satisfied that "Bella" captures my infinite complexity.

Needy

So. I'm stretched out on the coffee table, the breeze from the window tickling the silky filaments of my guard hairs, when I am lifted from my reverie, and the table. I am draped over Squishy's lap and told I am, quote, such a beautiful cat, unquote. Having some self-respect, a concept to which Squishy seems a stranger, I remove myself back to the coffee table, accompanied by her pathetic, pouting whine. She calls me, quote, a terrible cat, unquote.

Sometimes I wish I could talk, because moments like this call for a "Sheesh!" or two.

Cuddle is visiting this week. She lugged in mounds of clothes that smell of another cat (rundown on said cat: young, foolish, sweet, short-haired, and, oh dear goodness, a tabby! This strikes deep.) Now she wants my attention, but I am not so sure I want to fraternize at the moment.

Humans are needy. I don't mind most of the time, and I understand that the human need to seek perfection in the form of cats is strong. But when Squishy and Cuddle both get it into their big, round heads to "love the cat," it can become tiresome, if not downright dangerous. I scratch, they drop, I bite, they toss. But really, they act like kittens who need to be fed every twenty minutes.

When Cuddle comes home, she wants to sleep with me. I used to sleep with her almost every night, sharing one of her pillows, purring in her ear. For some reason, I no longer can settle down with her, even at the risk of being shut in the mudroom all night. I think it might be because she wants me to nestle—under her arm, across her chest, next to her head—and I just can't do it anymore. Now that I have reached my full, sweet maturity, cuddling with Cuddle is a hot business. Squishy calls it being "ladies of a certain age" and comes with a lot of insulation. But does Cuddle understand? She does not.

Long ago, before Cuddle, Squishy, or mudrooms, I was a young nomad, which did not suit me at all. First Mama, then a cage in the vet's office to audition minions, another house, kittens, and back to the vet's office to wait for the minions that were meant for me. During this time, I observed that other cats were less particular than I was about being fondled. Some seemed needier than the humans, if such a thing is possible. Once I saw a young tom roll on his back so his stomach could be stroked. Yes, I know— shocking. It makes my back bone watery and my claws come out to think of it.

In any case, living at the vet's showed me some cats don't find the neediness of minions as vexing as I do. Perhaps it's because they are not as beautiful as I am, so must make compromises. Perhaps I am just a cat of greater sensitivity, not meant for the hurly-burly of constant handling by needy minions, but intended by nature to sit aloof on a sunny windowsill, bringing joy at a distance as I wash a fuzzy paw.

Squishy approaches again. Her wheedling cries touch me with pity. She scratches my chin, I smile at her. She calls me beautiful cat again. The coffee table has grown hard, the patch of sun has moved on. Her touch is light, her voice rich with love. Cuddle comes and rucks up the fur on my nose, just the way I like it.

Yes, I will sit on Squishy's lap. My nomad days are over.

Bird

Yesterday afternoon, I heard scritch-scratching from the woodstove. As she lay stupefied on the couch, Squishy was not even alive to the danger before I sprang to her aid.

I gazed in the stove's ashy window. Yes, it was there, lunch and threat all in one. A house finch, its incarnadine head stained with the blood of its spring-time rivals, knocked at the glass — vicious little brute.

I don't know why the birds come to challenge me. When the weather turns sweet and warm, they flutter down the long, black stovepipe and bang themselves about with avian aggression behind the stove window, trying to take over my house. I do not allow it.

Squishy is up now, making soppy noises at the sight of the bird. I instruct her to release it, stand back, and let me handle things. Never one to go the simple route if the complicated will do, Squishy leaves the room. When next I see her, she is removing the screen from the window nearest the fire box. This idiocy again! You keep the bird inside; you don't release it!

She returns and opens the top of the window. I can only hope that this is one of those rare birds who, like Squishy, prefers to complicate things and will fly away from the opening.

At times, I can only describe myself as stunned by the actions of minions. Stupefaction is the only sensible response to Squishy's next move. She picks me up and tosses me in the mudroom. She shuts the door.

When my brain unfreezes from this unthinkable, yet all too frequent, eccentricity, I come to two conclusions. One, if Squishy should find herself in the wild, given her basic misunderstanding of "keep the bird in," she would die without me. Two, a cat's inability to roll its eyes is a serious evolutionary flaw.

The finch has the sense that Squishy was born without. The woodstove door creaks open. Through the door, I can hear the flutter of wings and then nothing. Gone.

In the next instant, Squishy opens the door. I indulge the hope that the finch isn't really gone, only resting on a picture frame. Perhaps Squishy has recognized—at last—the natural order: bird trapped, cat eats.

But no. I search the room while Squishy watches, apologizing for "ruining my fun." If it was only that, and not the great struggle of our time.

It is good that hope springs eternal in the feline breast. I stare into the fire box, my back to the disappointing Squishy, and wait for the next springtime assault of the finches.

Fruit

Squishy hid the box of peaches from me just now. As I was getting down to the business of pawing the fat, round, sweet little darlings to release their ambrosial fragrance, she snatched it from the wooden counter and set it on the washing machine. Bereft, but too proud to show it, I gazed away. Was the washing machine really too crowded and slippery to pursue my lovely, lovely peaches? It was.

I began my pursuit of fruit with strawberries. One day as Squishy and Popcorn were filling the counters with bags of their varied and, quite frankly, often puzzling foodstuffs, the lower counter became full, so Squishy set a clear box up on the wooden counter. I watched them unpack with interest, when, in gentle wafts, came the scent of heaven.

I began to rub and rub on the edges of the box, leaving streamers of gossamer fur lodged in the air holes that allowed the ruby gems to breathe on me. Up to that point, I had reserved such passion for backpacks.

But there they were beneath the plastic, glittering with goodness, coy sparkles glistening from their plump, dimpled curves, life-giving crimson sweetness a thin membrane away, calling, calling, calling...
Where am I? What am I saying? Give me a moment. Religious experiences are not easy to recall with calmness.

I began to paw at the box, hoping to achieve full immersion by licking and nibbling.

Squishy, after watching me for a moment with her hands on her hips, shook her head, slipped the box from under me, and shoved it in the refrigerator.

Exit ecstasy.

Squishy scoffs at the idea that cats can't taste sweet things, as some misguided researchers have said.

At breakfast time, I help her focus by sitting on the newspaper laid out in front of her. At one time, Squishy believed I shouldn't sit on the kitchen table. I don't know where she gets such false ideas, but through gentle training and more free time than she has, I have convinced her of her error. Now that she been retrieved from the darkness of ignorance, when I gaze at her from atop the newspaper with my feet wrapped in my tail, she need not say a word, our communion runs so deep. Only when she gets up for some forgotten item does she speak. She points a finger at her cereal bowl and speaks low.

"Don't even think about it," she says.

She's absolutely right. These moments

go beyond thought. I focus on the bottom of the bowl and think of joys to come. My self-control is legendary.

When Squishy finishes her part of breakfast, she pushes the bowl to me. She has left a thin pool of milk at the bottom, and I lap up the oaten-flavored milk, hints of sweetness swirling around my tongue. I would like her to leave more, but she says milk upsets my fine internal balance — or as Rumble has trained Popcorn to say: "Mom, the cat has vomited!" — so I am only given a sampling every morning.

Sometimes, if life has reached its heights, she has put bananas or, yes, even strawberries on her cereal. Words fail me — you will have to stretch your imagination to encompass my joy.

Squishy finally realized my yearning and devotion to strawberries. She now cuts a piece of juicy goodness for me and lays it at my feet. I lick and lick. Sometimes, to get it in my mouth, Squishy has to hold it in the spire of her fingers—I have few quibbles with the natural world that has created me, since, after all, it has created me, but I could have used a prehensile lip to assist in my fruit eating. As with her cereal milk, she doesn't allow me much, not knowing how it will affect my delicate system. Through my persistence—I haven't had to stand on my head to get her attention, but I'm willing—I have sampled melons, peaches, kiwis, and plums, too.

Squishy brings a peach to the counter. I watch as she peels it, the rosy juice dripping into the bowl beneath it. Before she takes the slices away for herself, she gets a saucer and pours peach juice into it. She sets the saucer in front of me.

Peach juice tastes like perfect understanding.

Left

They left me! All of them! Squishy, Rumble and Popcorn, all gone. The endless hours, the hunger, the bereft, grief-stricken cat.

Better to have loved and lost? I don't think so.

Each of the five or six times I woke up the first day, I wandered the house, looking into corners, but it was useless, useless. In my despair, I even put my nose to the glass of the porch door to look at the tabby.

That night, the man from up the hill came to feed me and the awful tabby. He seems a nice man, petting me and talking to me, but he isn't mine. "Where are they?" I asked. The existential abyss opened by my question was too much for the man. He called me a good cat, which hardly covers it, and left.

I couldn't eat. A strange, empty worm worked itself up and down my insides, making food a cruel joke. Besides, the nice man didn't mash up my food like Squishy does.

The next morning the nice man let me outside, but no one let me back in, even when I scratched on the window screen. Usually when I do that, Squishy leaps up with a high-pitched bleat and opens the door.

After my eternity of suffering, Rumble came back that night, but he was alone. What had he done with Popcorn and Squishy? Wrong, all wrong.

Rumble and I by ourselves make for uneasy times. He set down food for me, even said a word or two in my direction, but Rumble has never understood or accepted the necessity of minionhood. That necessity is, of course, that the cat must be allowed on your lap for as long as she wants, told she is beautiful, stroked down her back exactly three times and no more, or scratched behind the ears for a good long time, but only when she is being held close against the body, upright and face to face, if she allows you to pick her up at all. When she doesn't, you make disappointed noises like musical notes to her ears, because the minion's lot is a heartbreaking one, but it is the one ordained by the great powers of Nature and therefore beautiful, so stop complaining.

Rumble has trouble with these basics, so on the third night of our isolation together, when he tried to pet me as I wound around his feet, I scratched him good and deep. With one swipe, I illuminated for him our relative positions in the hierarchy of the universe.

Rumble has quite a throwing arm.

At last, Popcorn and Squishy couldn't stand life without me and came home.

I tried to ignore them, to punish them for abandoning me, but the smell of Popcorn's shoes made me feel all kawobbly. I had to rub them all over and put my face inside them, because they smelled of ancient rocks that pushed their way to the sun, then tumbled down again. They smelled of sharp-needled trees and cold, white water. I rubbed and rolled, drunk with this wild place Popcorn brought back with him.

Worse, I was helpless to ignore Squishy's lap that night. I tried, but her lap has a voice of its own, whispering warm and pillowy things. I managed to show my displeasure by avoiding eye contact as I curled up and swished my tail the entire time, but even as I swished, the purring started and wouldn't stop. It was as if another cat was in the room. I looked around for the terrible tabby, thinking she had somehow got in and was betraying cat solidarity with ill-advised purring, but it was me! Purr and swish, purr and swish, love and disgust each holding their own for a good hour.

Life has settled back into its routine since Squishy and Popcorn came back, but I suspect something is up. Squishy is bustling and bossing Popcorn. The suitcases have come out again.

The sweet ball of fluff maneuver is sure to keep her at home, so, excuse me, I have to go climb in a suitcase and look adorable.

Dog

Today, Squishy said we were in the "dog days of summer." I didn't know what she meant by that, because the pleasure of the hot day was unsullied by anything resembling a dog when we went out. Even the tabby baggage was so drunk with heat, she lay as if dead (if only) behind the potted plants. I sat on the patio table under the canopy and stared in the window, making Squishy think I wanted in. I had no intention of coming in, but her hopping up and down amused me.

When Squishy first let me out, I flopped down on the cement and wiggled, rubbing so I got a good face and back scratch. She always calls me "the white worm" when I do this. Of course, I'm not white at all, but a subtle, stunning cream color, darkening to the palest, shell-like orange at my face, paws and tail. Great drifts of hair billow around me, some of it wafting away on the breeze, some of it stroked off by Squishy, if I let her catch me. It sticks to her hands and arms, and her antics are almost as good as the rubbing: she says, "Gaah!" runs her hands up and down her arms, then shakes her fingers. My fur floats through the atmosphere like beautiful dreams.

But one should never be too complacent. The possibility always exists that some poor, deluded person will bring a dog past the house, or the dogs might come rampaging on their own, like lunatics escaped from the asylum.

"Dog" people don't understand the natural order of their minionhood, so they take into their houses slobbering, slavering idiots. They intend to be what's called the alpha dog, though few of them succeed. Even in their idiocy, dogs are crafty. They will tear the curtains from the windows (as opposed to merely climbing and shredding them, the purpose for which they were intended), as well as claw out their own dog door and rip and chew couch cushions. Everyone knows couch cushions are best shredded over time, not the work of one destructive afternoon! Then dogs will look at their horrified keepers with a smile and a waving tail, and be taken for walks and to chase balls, all forgiven.

Tell-tale signs are that a dog once lived here, but Squishy redeemed herself before it was too late. One point of agreement between Rumble and me is that dogs should not be seen, heard, or sleeping in the mud room.

But that brings us to today: terrible tabby blotto behind the potted plants, me, tired of the patio table ruse, my nose in the cool grass, slaying bugs. Then up the road comes the nice, if misguided, lady from up the hill, bringing Squishy's newspaper from the mailbox and not just her little, ill-behaved, black dog, who we sneer at, but a great, golden brute, who could eat the tabby in one swallow. Strangely, I object to that idea.

The brute bore down on me before I knew what was happening. I rose up, my fur in a fierce nimbus around me, too late to turn tail and run. My time had come.

Then, beside me crackled a terrible hulk of stripes, her face cheek to cheek with mine, making us a four-eyed, double-tailed monster. She hissed and stalked toward the brute, teeth I didn't know she had jumping into view. I couldn't let her have all the glory, so I sidestepped forward, hissing, all my fur collecting power. The pointy-nosed brute acted as if he'd hit a wall, and he had—a wall of feline righteousness and retribution. He slowed, stopped and ran back to the lady as if he had not a base intention in the world.

Coward!

We watched him retreat up the hill, as he pretended he'd never seen us.

The stripey interloper is again blotto, I am gazing at leaves. Tonight, I don't think I'll slap her bottom when she comes in for dinner.

Bed

Rumble was not at home last night, so I let Squishy sleep with me. I didn't make her sleep in the mudroom, but shared her bed, because, to tell the truth, I'm not that crazy about the mudroom.

For as long as I can remember, any little late evening cuddle has turned into the shut door of the mudroom. I don't know why this is, because I'm a good sleeper, not rising for my minions' attention until 4:30 or 5:00 in the morning. But the shut door it is, unless my native cunning and stealth come into play, and I escape the nightly capture.

As you know, I used to sleep with Cuddle before she left home and her own cat found her. She liked close-up sleeping, as did I, but as I became a cat of superior insulation, I just couldn't settle in with the heat bath that was Cuddle. I know it hurt her feelings, but my comfort being paramount, she would weep and let me go, after only a half hour or so of my scratching at the door and complaining and escaping her clutches.

I have never slept with Rumble. Our relationship being fraught with conflicting goals, and his understanding shaky, I only get on the bed with Rumble when I elude capture, hide under his bed, and need a good laugh. He provides this when I jump on him. He leaps like a gazelle out of sleep, then growls like a bear who wants to eat me, but knows the indigestion wouldn't be worth it. As he carries me to the mudroom, none too skillfully, I purr, which seems to irk him.

I do wish he would let me nap with him, though. I've mentioned Rumble's handsome pelt, of which any cat would be proud, but he is also a superior napper, almost cat-like in his ability to conk out. On the days he is home, he disappears each afternoon, to emerge after a couple of hours with rosy cheeks and bright, dazed eyes. If he allowed me to share sleep with him, I know he would reach a deeper understanding of my beneficence and graciousness, but Rumble, sadly, is a great believer in the closed door, even in daytime.

I don't press the point, since I have an inkling that Rumble might use his long legs and wiry musculature to kick a nap companion if crossed. In a way, I have to admire yet another of his feline qualities: a crankiness that, even if inconvenient for me, he raises to a masterly level.

Sleeping with Popcorn I reserve for those times of restlessness and malaise that have no other outlet. I have only done it twice, since in general my life is a satisfying balance of contemplation and entertainment. But in difficult emotional waters, if Popcorn wakes up to find me on his bed, his attitude of reverential awe at finding me there snaps the universe back into its courses. I can say "Farewell, Ennui!" and leave to have a wash.

So we come to sleeping with Squishy. Like the passionate dance of gopher hunting or fur grooming, sleeping with Squishy encompasses the heights and depths, the best and worst, perfect love and perfect despair.

Too much, in other words, for this poor forum. Possess your souls in patience, then: more anon, more anon.

Couch

It may have been Squishy's finest hour. It involved two burly workmen, Squishy fluttering like a moth around them, and Rumble standing in the background saying, "That's not right!"

But right it was, and the new couch filled the family room with a cream-colored glow.

Squishy had to work hard to get me a new couch. I, in fact, didn't know Squishy could work that hard. Over the course of a year, she had moved from standing over the two old couches, waving a dismissive hand and speaking in dulcet, reasonable tones, to gesticulating like a rabid heron and screeching in registers only heard by the smallest of small birds. Rumble caused this escalation by standing over Squishy and waving a dismissive hand over our need for a new couch.

My home appears to be the place where old couches go to die. Each of the four couches in the house came from somewhere else, and I would see Squishy's eye begin to twitch sometimes when she stood back, hands on hips, to frown at them.

Of the two couches Squishy had in her sights, one had a certain amount of give and, if I rearranged pillows, could be slept on. Its tan cover, like dull brown fungus, was tolerable, yet not pleasing to the paws. Under the cover was ripped fabric, nubby and striped—leading me to wonder at Squishy's tolerance for the stripey outdoor cat, when the sight of these stripes filled her with such despair. In her early negotiations with Rumble, of which I did not approve on general principles—has she learned nothing? I sometimes capitulate, but never negotiate— she would gesture at the couch with an open hand, offering it to him with a great deal of scorn and the words, "Twenty-eight years!" These words increased in volume over the course of time, while Rumble kept up the pretense that he was being reasonable.

I only used the second couch as a thoroughfare when it stood in my way to somewhere else. The upholstery was roughly equivalent in comfort to my tongue. Human hides could be abraded straight down to the bone on that couch. Whenever they had cause to move it, its great weight would mean days of recovery for at least three minions. I stayed well away when the brave souls removed the cushions, since the weight of one could take down a healthy cow, never mind a delicate feline like me.

Squishy often pondered over this couch, which came from her grandmother, about how old it actually was and if horse hair stuffing made it so unyielding. All I know is that I get echoing generations of cats from that couch, along with perfumes, smokes, cocktails and the boredom of children on long, dull afternoons.

Finally, Squishy wore Rumble down, after a multitude of times ticking off answers to his objections on her fingers, with the ticking off looking more and more is if her finger were an ax and the palm into which it was sunk his skull. Rumble, stubborn but not fool-hardy, decided that, yes, perhaps Squishy was serious about a new couch.

So it came, curving around the room like a paw being washed, exactly cat-colored.

Rumble finds it alarming that he can't always see me sleeping on the back of this couch. Perhaps some deep human memory of big cats stalking him through the grasses is awakened because of this cream-colored camouflage. He'll stare at me blending into the velvety upholstery and accuse Squishy of only buying the couch to make me happy.

To which I reply with a minion phrase as succinct and fraught with meaning as a meow: "Well, duh."

Vet

Squishy can be surprisingly tough-minded when it comes to inserting cats into yawning hell boxes.

Though something of an occupational hazard for cats, I shouldn't have been smug yesterday morning as Squishy stuffed the terrible tabby into the cat carrier of doom. No more than the motley midget deserves, I thought, to be hauled away and thrown into some howling abyss of pesky pests' labyrinthine netherworld of deserved despair and dusky, darkening, demonic…

Hold on. What was I saying?

Right. The tabby pest didn't put up any

struggle at all, being both naive and feeble-minded when it came to the perils of the box. I watched her, yes, with my own eyes, slide in without a claw in sight. My desire to bask in her plight fought with my shame that any cat could be so fatuous.

I watched the vehicle swallow the stripey whats-it and Squishy. It drove off. I began to relax, my queendom my own. Quiet reigned. All warm sleeping spots, inside and out, were mine alone. Ah, life, sweet life!

They were back in an hour. The little terror stumbled out of the blue box, dazed but whole, crushing all my hopes and dreams. Life, cruel life!

And this morning, I was stuffed into the self-same cat carrier of doom.

I put up more of a fight than the little ignoramus, my legs rigid and the rest of me a floppy mass of civil disobedience. All right, not so civil. I don't know that I drew blood, since my claws were busy becoming one with the fibers of the carpet, but I had Squishy wishing she'd never started the whole, ill-advised business.

Her grip slackened once or twice, but her brute strength prevailed. The door slammed shut and it was all over. I was going to die.

Not quietly, though.

I began to yowl my death chant, hoping it would be Squishy's death I was foretelling, not my own. I explored the full range and volume of yowling, from "I hate you" and "Curse your children's children" to loud, louder, loudest. As I grew fatigued, "Please allow me to live," and "Life is too sweet to leave it," snuck in, but all Squishy had to say was, "We'll be there in fifteen minutes."

As if that would comfort me. There? Where there? The labyrinthine netherworld of feline death?

As I bounced and swayed in the vehicle, Squishy turned a knob, and music came on.

I found it distracting and used it as a chance to rest my voice. Someone with a voice like Rumble sang, "Everywhere I go, the more I see, the less I know."

I say, "The more I see, the less I like it."

After months of travel, we arrived at the place where the mishmash of smells would make any right-thinking cat hunker down and try to become invisible, so I did. Squishy set the carrier on a bench. An orange cat sashayed past, smirking. A rangy gray beast slithered past as well, insinuating himself under the benches. Realizing they were demons disguised as cats, I let out a low growl.

I growled again when Squishy took me to a little room with all the air sucked out of it. If the cat carrier of doom was bad, I knew the cold metal table was worse, so again I went floppy. Curse the persistence of minions! The neck grab can't be fought forever.

The neck-grabber put me on a shallow dish and ignored my volcanic rumble. When I was dragged off the dish, I heard the word "chunky," but blocked out the rest.

I'll spare you the details of the poking, prodding, and sticking that went on. They were experts there: I didn't get in a single stick of my own. Shoved back into the box of terror, heaved up and out to the car, I began my death chant again. After a few sympathetic coos, Squishy was infected with the general heartlessness of the place.

"Oh, for Pete's sake," she said and turned the music on. I played dead, hoping Squishy would be torn asunder with grief. She wasn't.

We got home. I was released. I lived, no thanks to Squishy. The tabby terror sniffed at me, no doubt rejoicing inside, until I whacked her face.

My one consolation was the red warning label on the blue box of death, a warning to all the pokers, prodders and stickers.

"Take care! Cat bites!"
You bet I do.

Chase

This is War. The tabby twit is terrified, her claws clattering down the tile hallway as she seeks to escape the wrath that is me.

To set the scene: I am minding my own business, deep in my morning exercise, chasing my feather chicken. Now and then, after I subdue the chicken and before it makes another run for it, I treat Squishy to some play time, batting her ankles as she passes by. She squeals with delight when I do this and hurries about her work with renewed energy.

I rest a paw on the chicken's brown back, considering whether I should attack the edge

of the rug, when the pest walks past, swishing her tail in an insolent manner. I have just conquered a chicken; I'm not going to put up with this provocation from a mere striped vagabond.

I levitate off the chicken and sidestep on stiff legs toward the pest. She slows. She turns with a hop, aware now of her danger. She puffs up, twice her normal size. Do I let that stop me? I do not.

She lifts off the floor and scampers past me down the hall. I barrel after her, full of energy and power. Do I think she will escape? I do not.

As I careen through the living room doors after her, I come whisker to whisker, her orangey eyes boring into me, the centers black pits of wickedness. I decide it's time to wear her down by outrunning her. Out I go through the living room doors, my furry paws slipping on the tile. Now I have her where I want her.

We repeat, changing routes, sliding into Squishy's legs once, the pest banging her head on a table leg once. I hook my claw in the rug and almost lose my advantage before tearing it free from sheer strength of will. Nothing, not even a berber carpet, can oppose me for long.

I make my stand in the center of the family room. Yes! She sidles toward me, puffy and frightened, ears laid back to threaten me. But I am supreme! I am all-powerful! I am the crystal-eyed lion whose stare shatters the infidel!

We circle, lifting paws in infinitesimal increments, then set them down again and lift the other. We lash tails and rumble in a wave length that shakes the foundations of the house.

This goes on for some time.

Then the pest's ears perk toward a bird outside the window. She licks the back of her paw.

I notice I'm a little peckish and would like a snack. I look around the room as the pest points her back leg at me and washes that. I think I have taught her who's in charge, so I back away, gazing into a corner of the ceiling.

She sashays out of the room toward her spot on the living room couch. After a quick nosh, I wander through to the living room couch as well, thinking I would like a change of scene today. The tabby twit is curled in a ball on one end.

I jump up on the other end of the couch, but she doesn't stir. I groom my back and tail, then find the time is right for a little nap. I tuck my paws under me and drowse with my nose on the upholstery. The twit flicks an ear in her sleep.

This is Peace.

Same

Person is too slow in the morning, and I must become cranky with her to speed things up. This was not always so. But now I am hungry and she must feed me.

Many things have changed for me.

Some days I sleep inside from morning until night. I like a different place to sleep now, not the chair under the table, but on one end of the white couch in the big, quiet room.

I will share this place with Person. I like to share it with her. She pets me, and the petting is so nice, I have to lick my chops. It is embarrassing to drool, but the petting feels so good, the water starts. I jump down and rub her legs and the short table legs and the edge of the couch, then I begin again and rub some more. I jump up beside her head and walk back and forth, looking down at her. Sometimes I settle on the back of my couch, looking at her and looking out the window at the same time. It is good beyond anything.

She lays down with me sometimes with no covering on her feet. I like to rub against them. When I lick them, she curls and uncurls them and makes a funny little floating sound. Then they look so sweet, I chew on them. If I do not chew hard, she lets me and says, "You little devil."

Sometimes she says, "Ouch."

Big Person comes and sits down and makes rumbling sounds on my couch. Rumble, quiet, rumble, quiet. He is so close and Person likes him. His rumbling almost sounds like purrs, so I get up and turn on my back beside him. I stretch out a paw and pet him, then roll and wiggle. I use my nose and find his hand and put my paws around it. I get up and stand on his leg. I look into his face and prove to him that he is a most interesting person. Finally, without stopping his rumble, quiet, rumble, quiet, he scratches behind my ears and runs his big, heavy hand down my back. My back rises to meet his hand and we are a match.

Person watches us and calls me a flirt. Big Person says it's nice to have a cat that likes to be petted. I think that means he has lately tried to pet Big Fluff and had bad luck with it.

Sweet Person comes to see us sometimes. She talks to me in cat, better than Person, and she made me brave enough to sit with her on Big Fluff's couch in the noisy room. Now I mosey through the noisy room to Big Fluff's water bowl or wander around it looking for action or sometimes curl up with Person and Big Fluff on that couch. Yes, I know this will be a big surprise, but Big Fluff looks down at me from the back of her couch just as I look down at Person on my couch, as if I am a most interesting amusement for her, and good company.

I have learned that doors open in the day if I sit beside them. I like to go in and out. Person talks to me when I do. I have heard her say, "Good God, now it's two of them," or "You're a proper house cat now, aren't you?"

Big Person says I now have my staff, but I don't know what that means. Maybe that I will be fed and petted, no matter what.

I put myself out at night, because Person does it otherwise and I do not like that picking-up stuff. So I walk to the door when she opens it and go into the cool night. Since I sleep inside in daytime, I am ready for smells and secrets and gophers when I go out. I know the door will open for me in the morning.

I walk through to my bowl, touching noses with Big Fluff on the way, fighting off her paw with mine. This is my house, too, and these are my people. Even Big Fluff is mine now, and I am hers.

Nap

Squishy is a bad napper. She joined me upstairs as I napped today, but as much as I like to see her, my joy at sharing sleep is sheer delusion. Squishy is a nap-whiner.

Napping for Squishy is a drawn out process, taking up to two weeks. To begin with, she spends three or four days moping around the house, moaning about how tired she is. After this painful interval, she'll lay down one afternoon (or lie down, but what does it matter? You know what I mean) and start to thrash, accompanied by petulant little snorts and sighs. She twists and bends as if in the throes of a catnip craze. She lasts about ten minutes before opening a book or leaping out of bed with an anguished cry. Squishy is easily bored, which is perhaps the worst part of being human or being Squishy. Or being Squishy's cat overseer.

If she lasts longer than that, settling into a doze and making her stomach available to me for colonizing, she still feels the need for some action. This action she finds by mauling me, petting me over and over and over, even up to three or four times in a half hour. The whole point of her napping—making me happy and warm—becomes moot.

For Squishy to take a nap like a normal person, i.e., a cat, calls for a stringent set of requirements. Though, come to think of it, "a stringent set of requirements" would make her naps so uncatlike that they can hardly be called by the name. My only requirement, and I think I speak for all cats, is closed eyes. Sometimes not even that, though that's a little eerie.

Anyway, requirements: the moping, failed attempts at bed napping, a couch, a book, the simultaneous lowering of book and eyelids. When I join her, she purrs, lays her hand on my back, but doesn't pet. When optimal nap conditions are met, she can snore there for up to two hours, scarcely moving a muscle. All is peace.

To give Squishy credit, sleeping with her at night is a different thing. I get to do this when she somehow detaches herself from Rumble, either by sending him off somewhere for a few days, by bringing germs home to make him sick, or by getting sick herself. Then, bidding each other adieu with false protestations of regret and scarcely contained glee, they take to separate beds. I follow Squishy into hers, after waiting a suitable time to see if her intentions include tossing me into the mudroom and slamming the door. I can be certain she's down for the night when she has her book open. After that, nothing short of curling smoke and leaping flames will shift her.

Though she's not a great sleeper, even at night, Squishy whines less and purrs more at night. In summer, I sleep on one corner of the bed, but in winter, after she turns out the light and flops on her stomach to sleep, Squishy makes a nest for me between her knees, or in the crook of her legs. I don't let her shoving me away deter me from curling up close to her, again and again if necessary, until she settles for the night. The cozy comfort of it makes me vibrate with pleasure just thinking about it.

Sometimes I think it's strange that the sweetest times sleeping with Squishy are when she's not asleep. Deep in the night, or when she has lain quiet for a long time, she will turn and circle her arm around my back. She'll bury her face in the silk under my chin and lay without a sound for a minute, maybe two. She goes back to her pillow; soon I hear her sleeping breath sigh close to me. Then I know she needs me, and I've done my duty. The night closes around us, holding us in its peaceful hands.

Gone

The pest has been gone a week now. The first few days, Squishy stood outside the front door and called her. Here, kitty, kitty. Here, Shy-shy.

The next mornings, she just stepped outside and looked up and down the hill.

The last two mornings, she has only opened the door a tabby-sized crack, then quickly closed it, as if the sight of the door mat stings her.

The absence of the stripey ruffian causes me a strange disquiet. What will I bat to show I am queen but her furry behind? What do you mean, here is my food? She gets her food first. That is the way it is.

Once morning is over, it is not so hard for me—she would sleep in her room, I would sleep in mine. But today, Squishy cannot stop the water. Not the crashing storm I have seen before. This water is quiet, a well rising up and spilling over.

Tonight, I will sit behind Squishy on our couch and wash her head. Tomorrow morning, I will bat at her ankles as she passes to remind her that someone is still here.

Even a small sorrow is still a sorrow.

Fine

"Hey, Kitty,

You're so fine,

You're so fine you blow my mind.

Hey, Kitty (uh, uh).

Hey, Kitty (uh, uh)."

Popcorn's chant would be flattering, if it wasn't so irritating.

Serene

I am serene today. I'm sitting in a patch of sun on the tip of my couch. A tranquil, velvety goodness strokes me. I gaze out at the trees. I don't want to go out. I want nothing. I want for nothing. I am serene.

This feeling doesn't come often for cats or minions from what I've seen. Being dead asleep, though a desirable state, isn't the same as this cushiony, floaty being.

Often I'm restless. In, out, up, down, company, solitude: I can't decide. So I try them all, especially in and out.

Rumble sometimes looks at me and wonders what I'm thinking. Squishy sometimes tries to supply an answer. Both of them conclude that I don't think about much. How wrong they are.

I have so much to think about. The usual daily things like food, comfy spots, chasing rubber bands inside or waving grass outside, tracking down Squishy behind closed doors, going outside and going inside occupy my mind.

Then the greater questions arise, such as why are dogs allowed, will Squishy ever leave me, what did she need with another cat, was the pest playing or attacking, is there any love greater than Squishy's?

Most days are filled with these thoughts. You wonder why cats sleep so much? You would too if you indulged is such arduous mental labors.

Squishy sits down with her book, the patch of sun surrounding us. Before she reads, she turns and runs her finger from my nose up to my ears. We look at each other for a long moment, as those who understand each other look.

Then there it is: the drop of water from her eye, as she looks at me, but thinks of another.

On the floor, in that leaping mote of dust in the sun, the little pest walks past, her curled tail like a question mark she no longer needs. Her stripes ripple as she passes in and out of the sun, glossy and fine.

I jump down and bat the shadow that was she, for old time's sake. I pounce and put my ears back, fierce, but the shadow goof rubs against my face.

Squishy thinks I'm batting at nothing.

I wish I could tell her. Shadows sit with her. Little ones with long tails, darting in and out, sit up to look at her. A big yellow beast lies at her feet. A shadow cat, so like the pest, curls up on Rumble's lap as he reads. And shadow people are here, looking at her with love.

Another drop falls, but Squishy rests her head on her arm and smiles at me.

"Silly cat," she says.

Squishy turns to her book and opens it. I jump up again and settle behind her. She reaches backward once to scratch my forehead, her arm, like the sun rising, in a delicate arc. I nod off in the bright sun to the gentle sigh of Squishy's finger sliding between the pages. Sometimes it is a bad old world, but now—perfect place, perfect world, perfect love.